ARANZI MACHINE GUN
vol. 3

Mr. Sprite's
Voyage
~Viet Nam~

Việt Nam T.P. Hồ Chí Minh

There were two reasons
I went to Vietnam:
First, to see my old friend Raccoon Dog.
And second, I just had to try on
one of those cone hats.

I had a shirt tailor-made just for me.
They took my measurements and made
the shirt with fabric selected at the mar
It only took two days.
I tried it on right away: a perfect fit!

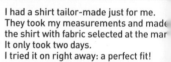

First of all, some sight-seeing. Rode a cyclo.

Bought a cone hat. Also bought some souvenirs.

Sent some postcards.

Met with Raccoon Dog. We hadn't seen each other in ages. Seems he's running a boat service on the Mekong River. He had a rich, dark tan.

He's been a vagabond for a long time, but recently settled down here. "I'll just go where the river takes me."

"You've come all this way. You should watch the sun set on the Mekong."

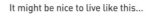

It might be nice to live like this...

"A perfect smoke."

In My Toh, a town in the Mekong Delta, just outside of Ho Chi Minh City.
02 Feb 2004

Here I am with Mr. Shindo of T & T Travel,
who took good care of me while I was there.

That was a good trip...
Now I should go take these souvenirs to
Spritekin and Fish.

Panda Field Guide

Edited by Panda, Ph.D. in Panda Studies

The Panda Bug

These bugs come out of the earth in Spring.
They can breed in your bathroom and blankets too, you know.

The Panda Bird

This highly evolved bird can travel on land, sea, and air.
If you tame the Panda Bird, it will perch on your hand.

The Panda Fish

Tasty when broiled with salt.
The black Panda Fish don't taste good, though,
so don't get the two confused.

The Panda Flower

If you water them, they're happy.
If you don't water them, they get angry and bite.

The Panda Fungus

If you get infected, the skin around your eyes will turn black and you'll turn into a panda.

Miscellaneous Panda

There are all kinds of other pandas in the panda family:

Panda Octopus

Panda Turtle

Panda Mushroom

Panda Frog

Panda Dinosaur

Panda Ghost

Panda Rabbit

Panda Cat

Panda Person

Terry, can I nestle up to you?

Terry, can I climb on top of you?

Hey, Little Terry, now you're getting carried away

Belt ·Pinkie·

I've been into belts lately

I wrap one around,

squeeeeeze real tight,

and make a waist for myself!

Making Ugly Faces ·Panda and Mechani-panda·

You're like, really good looking, Panda.

Oh yeah?

It's actually kind of unfair. You should try making an ugly face.

No way!

C'mon! You have to. Just this one time, please?

Ugh..... You're such a pain! Okay, just this once.

Heh

Fart · Sprite Kong and Spritekin ·

Being so embarrassed about just a fart.....
Spritekin saw a side to Sprite Kong he never knew was there.

Pose ·Birdie·

False Information 1 · White Rabbit ·

False Information 2 • Black Sheep •

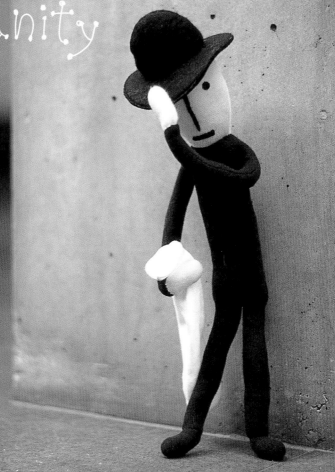

Fashion Vanity

Kidnapper has a monotone style.
The chic black suit and white kidnapping bag
give him personality.

Slim Boy fancies a bright pullover.
His effortless style gets the ladies' attention.

Skeleton keeps it real with his punk fashion.
His brand of cool is hard to imitate.

...a glittering costume.
A drag queen with a gorgeous smile.

Denim Boy naturally styles it in denim.
His way to fashion mastery is denim-on-denim.

35

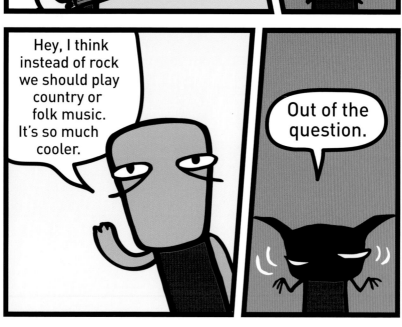

Having realized that girls would die without cute stuff, White Rabbit and Brown Bunny organized a "Cute Stuff Expedition" and set off.

49

He's so cool... I think I'm falling in love

Skirt

I don't really like skirts.

I prefer pants.

When I wear pants, I can do stuff like this...

or even this.

It makes
me feel

like I can go to
all sorts of
places.

Oh, but

I love
this cute
dress.

You can make all sorts of cute stuff with cute fabrics.
Even if it's a simple pattern and easy to make, if you make it with cute fabrics, look!
It's still cute! Try it out!

Make Cute Stuff With Cute Fabrics

Instructions on pages 72 - 75

Tote Bag

This tote bag can be used for school, work, or shopping as a second bag.
It's so convenient!
Since it's a second bag, you can use silly fabrics and it will still be adorable!

55

Tissue Box Cover

Make Mr. Tissue Box a suit out of cute fabric and voilà! Super! He'll stand out magnificently as a stylish object or part of the décor.

Lunch Bag and Cup Satchel

When you see cute fabrics, don't you just want to make a little drawstring purse? What, you don't? But if you *were* going to make a little purse, why not for something in particular? I got it! Let's make a lunch bag and a cup satchel! Perfect! Now try making satchels for all sorts of things.

Weird Dolls

How would you feel about having mice and skeletons and birds
printed all over your body and face? Gross!
But it might actually be kind of fun.
These weird dolls don't seem to mind at all.
It makes them happy and excited.

Miss Appliqué's
Magic
I'm Miss Appliqué.
What shall we appliqué today? Hmm.....
How about making appliqués of the Aranzi gang?
I'll use just a touch of my magic.
Easy-to-understand instruction and patterns included, of course!

The Bunnies showed up just in time! Appli-pli-pli-pli-Pliqué!! Watch,

Let's see,
who's next?
I guess it's
your turn.

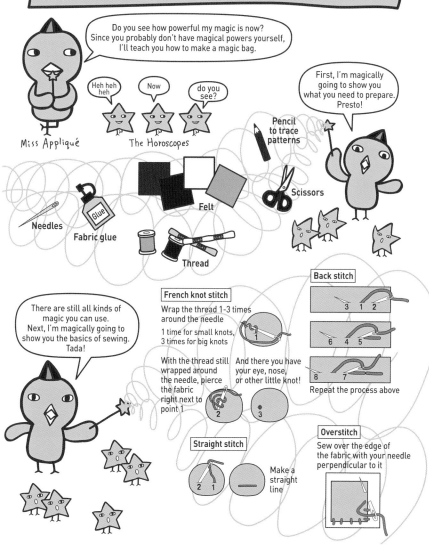

by Miss Appliqué

How to make Magic Bags

Do you see how powerful my magic is now? Since you probably don't have magical powers yourself, I'll teach you how to make a magic bag.

Heh heh heh

Now

do you see?

Miss Appliqué

The Horoscopes

First, I'm magically going to show you what you need to prepare. Presto!

Pencil to trace patterns

Scissors

Needles

Glue

Fabric glue

Felt

Thread

There are still all kinds of magic you can use. Next, I'm magically going to show you the basics of sewing. Tada!

French knot stitch

Wrap the thread 1-3 times around the needle

1 time for small knots, 3 times for big knots

With the thread still wrapped around the needle, pierce the fabric right next to point 1

And there you have your eye, nose, or other little knot!

Straight stitch

Make a straight line

Back stitch

3 1 2

6 4 5

8 7

Repeat the process above

Overstitch

Sew over the edge of the fabric with your needle perpendicular to it

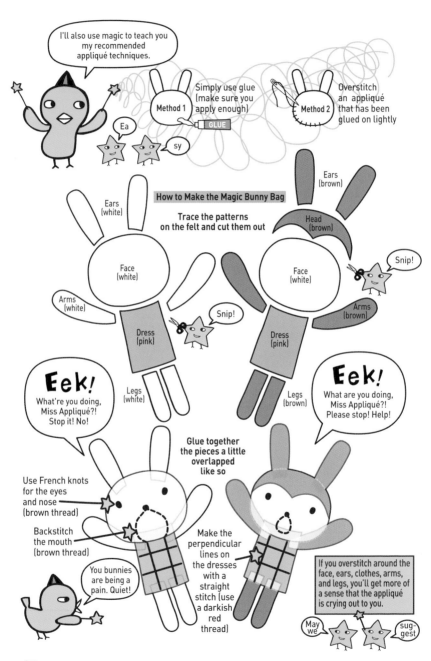

68

How to Make the Sprite and Spritekin Magic Bag

1. Trace the patterns on the felt and cut them out

Plate (brown)

Snip!

Plate (light brown)

Face (blue-green)

Face (green)

Mouth (white)

Mouth (white)

Arms (blue-green)

Body (blue-green)

Arms (green)

Body (green)

Snip!

Snip!

Legs (blue-green)

Legs (green)

2. Glue together the pieces a little overlapped like so

Line up the plate with the edges of the head and glue on

Huh?

What is this? Miss Appliqué, what have you done?

Sprr?

Sprite? Sprite, sprite sprite? Spriiiite?

French knot stitch the nose (brown thread)

Make the arms look like he's surprised

French knot stitch the eyes (black thread)

The line in the mouth should be straight stitched

He doesn't

get it

If you overstitch around the face, body, arms, and legs, they will look even more surprised.

Sprite and Spritekin have been turned into magic bag appliqués... but they still don't seem to get it, hee hee hee!

May we

sug-gest

1. Trace the patterns on the felt and cut them out

Whites of eyes (white)

Mouth (white)

Snip!

Face (black)

Arms (black)

Clothes (red)

Snip!

Snip!

Snip!

Legs (black)

2. Glue together the pieces a little overlapped like so

French knot stitch the pupils

No   es   cape

Scram!

No way I'm going to be caught! Escape is victory!

The white of eyes and mouth are very narrow, making an overstitch difficult. Be especially careful to apply enough glue

If you overstitch around the face, body, arms, and legs, he'll seem to be running

May we   sug-gest

Now, now, Bad Guy... you can't run away, can you?

If you want to be able to use magic, you have to practice. Like this:

Appli-pli-pli -pli-pliqué!!

I think daily practice should help. Actually, you might as well not even try.

Not   even   try

How To
Make Cute Stuff
With Cute Fabrics

Tote Bag

These instructions will show you how to make a large tote bag (27 cm tall x 29 cm wide). You can make all kinds of bags of different sizes, though. You can become a tote bag expert!

You Need:
- Fabric
- Pencil or something else to draw with
- Scissors
- Sewing machine (or needle if you don't have one)
- Ruler
- Thread
- A sewing machine that can do zig-zag or overlock stitches (if available)

First, cut the fabric. Then, run the edge of the fabric under a zig-zag or overlock machine to prevent it from fraying.

Bag: Fabric, 1 sheet
66 x 31 cm

Handles: Fabric,
2 pieces, 32 x 8 cm

Fold in both edges of the handles about 1 cm.

← Reverse

Then fold the handles in half lengthwise.

← Front

Once folded, sew along both edges.

← Front

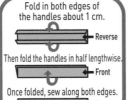

---

5 cm

8.5 cm
3 cm
8 cm
8 cm
3 cm
8.5 cm

Cut four 3 cm slits into your bag.

These slits will make it much easier to insert the handles later.

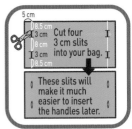

Fold the fabric for the bag in half, with the interior facing out, and sew 1 cm in along the edges.

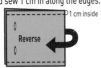

1 cm inside

Reverse

If you have a sewing machine, use that. Otherwise, just sew by hand.

Reverse

Now turn the bag inside out.

Front

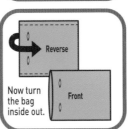

Fold out the opening of the bag about 5 cm.

5 cm

Front

Reverse

Insert the handles as shown into the slits.

Reverse   Front

Let the ends of the handles stick out about 0.5 cm from the slits.

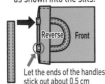

Sew across the opening 1cm from the edge of the slits.

Then unfold and turn out the opening like this.

Reverse

Front

Front

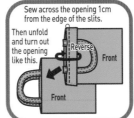

Now sew along the opening of the bag 1 cm from the edge, and your bag is complete.

Sew across, 1 cm inside

You can now go out and use it right away!

Front

72

Tissue Box Covers

Tissues are also called nose wipes or paper handkerchiefs.
But you won't call them that once they're in a tissue case—they'll be tissues.
(Tissue box case instructions are for tissue boxes measuring 11.5 cm wide x 24 cm long x 5.5 cm tall.)

You Need:

- ● Fabric ● Ruler ● Thread
- ● Pencil or other drawing material ● Sewing machine (or needle if you don't have one)
- ● Scissors ● Cardboard
- ● A sewing machine that can do zig-zag or overlock stitches (if available)

Let's start with the pocket tissue case. First cut the cardboard.

Cardboard,
1 sheet
9 x 14 cm

"What's this for?" you're probably asking yourself. It'll come in handy later.

Cut the fabric.

Fabric,
1 sheet
14 x 21.5 cm

Run the edges of the fabric under a zig-zag or overlock-stitch machine.

Fold in both edges 1 cm, then sew the edge 0.7 cm in.

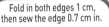

① Fold 1 cm

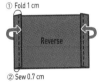

Reverse

② Sew 0.7 cm

Place the cardboard at the center of the fabric. Fold in both edges of the fabric over the cardboard.

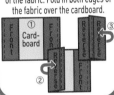

Pull out the cardboard and sew along the top and the bottom, 1 cm in.

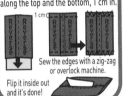

1 cm

Sew the edges with a zig-zag or overlock machine.

Flip it inside out and it's done!

All refreshed, now let's make a tissue box case. First, cut the fabric.

Fabric, 2 sheets
13.5 x 38 cm

Sew the edges with a zig-zag or overlock machine.

With the insides facing out, sew the tops of the two sheets together.

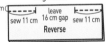

1 cm | leave
sew 11 cm | 16 cm gap | sew 11 cm
Reverse

Don't sew the 16 cm portion in the center. That's the opening for the tissues.

Now open it up and fold the hems in to the reverse side. Sew across 0.7 cm in from the edge.

Did you get this?

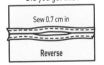

Sew 0.7 cm in

Reverse

Fold triangles out of the four corners of your fabric and sew them shut.

6 cm

Reverse

Does it look like this with the corners sewn?

Reverse

Cut the ends off the four corners and run the edges through zig-zag or overlock machine.

2 cm

Reverse | Reverse

Reverse

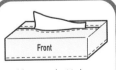

Front

It's convenient to have a lot of tissue boxes around the house. Just be careful not to waste tissues!

Lunch Bag and Cup Satchel

Make a delicious lunch and put it in your lunch bag when you go out.
Put your favorite cup in the cup satchel then take it with you.
But what would an adult do with a cup? Just a pain to carry around?

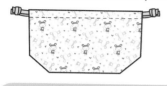 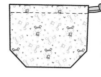

The lunch bag is
15 cm wide x 10 cm gusset x 14 cm tall
The cup satchel is
9 cm wide x 9 cm gusset x 14 cm tall

You Need:
● Fabric   ● Ruler   ● Something to draw with   ● Scissors
● Sewing machine (or needle if you don't have one)   ● Thread   ● Drawstrings
● A sewing machine that can do zig-zag or overlock stitches (if available)

Let's start with the lunch bag.

| Fabric, 2 sheets 23 x 28 cm | So that the edges of the fabric don't fray |

Cut two pieces of fabric and run the edges under a zig-zag or overlock machine.

Overlay the two sheets with the insides facing out. Sew 1 cm inside along the edges, leaving the top 6 cm open.

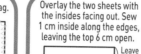

Leave 6 cm open

Sew 1 cm in

---

① Fold in the four corners of the top a little, like this.

Reverse

② Then fold over the edges 2.5 cm.

③ Sew along the edges, 2 cm in.   Reverse

Now make the gusset in the bottom. Flatten both bottom edges and sew 10 cm across.

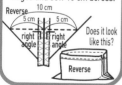

Reverse   10 cm
5 cm   5 cm
right angle   right angle

Does it look like this?

Reverse

Flip inside out, and insert drawstrings. Tie the strings and you have a finished lunch bag.

Front

Front

Now for the cup satchel. Cut the fabric and run the edge under a zig-zag or overlock machine. Fold the fabric, inside facing out, and sew.

Fabric, 1 sheet 22 x 38 cm

Leave 6 cm open

Reverse

Fold over
① the two corners of the top a little, just as with the lunch bag.

Reverse

② Then fold over the edges 2.5 cm.

③ Sew along 2 cm from the top.

Reverse

Now make the gusset in the bottom. Flatten both bottom edges and sew 9 cm across.

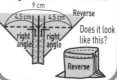

9 cm
4.5 cm   4.5 cm   Reverse
right angle   right angle

Does it look like this?

Reverse

Turn it inside out and insert a drawstring. Tie the ends and you have a cup satchel!

Front

Front

 Weird Dolls

Is it a bear? A ghost? What is it? Weird. That's why they're called weird dolls.
We recommend making them out of character prints like these.

You Need: ● Fabric ● Pencil or something to draw with ● Scissors ● Sewing needle ● Sewing machine (if you have one) ● Thread ● Felt ● Cotton

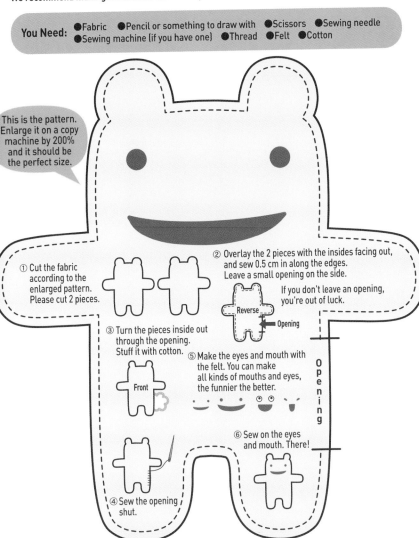

This is the pattern. Enlarge it on a copy machine by 200% and it should be the perfect size.

① Cut the fabric according to the enlarged pattern. Please cut 2 pieces.

② Overlay the 2 pieces with the insides facing out, and sew 0.5 cm in along the edges. Leave a small opening on the side.

If you don't leave an opening, you're out of luck.

Reverse — Opening

③ Turn the pieces inside out through the opening. Stuff it with cotton.

Front

⑤ Make the eyes and mouth with the felt. You can make all kinds of mouths and eyes, the funnier the better.

Opening

⑥ Sew on the eyes and mouth. There!

④ Sew the opening shut.

When
we think of
Tokyo,
we think of
Tokyo
Tower.

When I think of Nagoya, I think of chicken wings.

When we think of Sapporo, we think of snow.

Let's cuten things up with The Cute Book

$12.95/$16.00 CND

Full of patterns and introductions to characters.

They're easy to make and easier to love.

The Bad Book stars the one and only Bad Guy, along with his unbelievably bad friend, Liar.

$12.95/$16.00 CND

You want to see a really bad book?

No.

Meet the new generation of pet-sized Aranzi dolls!

Making the Aranzi mascots was easy enough,
but are you ready to have a cute doll to call your own?
They're bigger and require a little extra love, but not much more—
just enough to give them a life of their own.

Aranzi
Cute Dolls
Large format, 80 pages
October 2007, $14.95/$19.95C

Aranzi
Fun Dolls
Large format, 80 pages
October 2007, $14.95/$19.95C